Wall Street Mortgage

Cancellation Secrets

"What Smart Rich People Don't Tell and Big Banks Will Steal To Not Let You Know"

Powerful Techniques To Rescind and Cancel Mortgages

(New Format Update)

KYLE RANSOM

Dedications

All my family members and closest friends...Beautiful wife and daughter!

Every original purchaser of the Ransom Foreclosure Profit System, QWR Attack!, Common Law Lien Review, Go Fight Foreclosure Profit System and Go Fight Foreclosure Profit System 2.0.

Contents

Intro

Inside gain knowledge for the most resourceful techniques to properly rescind and cancel mortgages because of mortgage securities fraud. This material can help any borrower, you don't need to be behind or facing foreclosure to benefit. It's not required that you go to court to enforce the techniques in this material to rescind and cancel mortgages. It's exactly the kind of knowledge you have been searching for explained quick and simple.

Why is this material so significant right now for the American people? When I was in the military serving in the best branch of the U.S. Navy it was under top secret specialty clearance. I understood what the wrong people could do if they ever got their hands on important information. From that experience I learned that "knowledge is power" and why using knowledge of secret information can even disrupt a world.

So what if "good people" could get their hands on powerful information that could possibly change their financial situation? A family struggling to pay their mortgage and upside down in the loan could reorganize! A homeowner facing foreclosure could turn the tables on the lender and negotiate a better resolution.

Are these promises? No, no one can promise you anything and if they do run! What I am offering you is knowledge and knowledge is the most enforceable power to demand what you want or need for your specific financial circumstances.

The powerful knowledge in this material exposes how a homeowner can shift positions on the lending industry Goliath! My 16 years of mortgage industry experience and seasoned 20 plus years of expert mortgage securities knowledge focuses how to gain clear and quiet title using practical techniques without going to court! Have the original mortgage loan down payment and every payment ever made returned plus with interest on every single payment including the original escrow by collapsing the bonds it was built on...

Are you awake and did I get your attention? Only you have the power to take this knowledge to use it and change your current situation so purchase this material right now to make it happen.

My Purpose

Maybe I'm writing this material because I wasn't born into the Kardashian Jenner clan and can't get paid for my socialism influence. See I learned that information from my wife about socialism influence, which she better understands influential marketing with her background in sociology better than I do...no the real reason I'm writing this material is because after my first bestselling book on home foreclosure big banks are still getting away with stealing homes from families but just differently today after many newer cases and restructuring after foreclosure cases were decided in higher courts. It was evident that I needed to provide those struggling with mortgages they can't afford or under the threat of foreclosure with updated current information beyond The Home Foreclosure EBook!

I discovered that I may have had characteristics of reality stars and I hate reality television (sorry for those who love reality tv don't mean to offend anyone) but I may have exposed my fight with foreclosure in a reality manner long before it became a popular obsession. When I launched The Home Foreclosure Ebook in 2013, it was from the knowledge of my previous information products the Ransom Foreclosure Profit System, Go Fight Foreclosure System and later Go Fight Foreclosure System 2.0 my greatest gifts to homeowners fighting and challenging foreclosures at that time. Especially those starting their foreclosure fight around the year of 2007 which was when my own personal foreclosure journey started. In reality style manner I disclosed my personal information about my challenges with fighting home foreclosure. As a former mortgage broker catering to investors over traditional homebuyers, I was very familiar with challenging foreclosures successfully for many years but not on my personal home apart from investment properties I had owned.

I put my personal information out there as an effort to help other homeowners understand that dealing with foreclosure was nothing to be ashamed of or even embarrassed about. So then others facing foreclosure could see someone else just like them. It was a saving grace for banks who relied on borrowers being shamed by foreclosure and a primary reason most homeowners didn't challenge their foreclosures even when they knew the banks lied about especially loan modifications and still foreclosed. My very first information product was the Ransom Foreclosure Profit System intended to educate entrepreneurs on how to successfully start a business assisting homeowners with loan modifications. My history with the foreclosure crisis goes way back... After being profiled in a major magazine about the Ransom Foreclosure Profit System my creditably really expanded across the nation.

The Go Fight Foreclosure System 2.0 had such a powerful impact for providing knowledge about securitization flaws that many homeowners did get free and clear titles to their mortgages following the techniques. These homeowners know exactly who they are and they were forced into confidentiality agreements to never ever discuss the terms. As for anyone such as a big bank wanting to know if a homeowner told me anything to show how the homeowner may have breached their confidentiality agreements ?? Please don't waste your time "I" am unaware of which homeowner or homeowners or settlement or settlements or document or documents you are referring to!

Never will I discuss any details of any foreclosure cases I have reviewed, EVER!! In fact I don't recall period and any foreclosure documents I reviewed are no longer in my possession or under my control... In short, this not my first time at the rodeo folks, lenders tried to squeeze me for years to not help homeowners fighting foreclosures. There were many attempts to discredit my expertise in understanding foreclosure related to mortgage securitization and harm me from making a living in this field. For those challenging times I thank them because it enabled me to launch other business models to diversify how I make a living even today. It made me a fierce businessman in varies sectors of different industries!

While the Go Fight Foreclosure System 2.0 continued to help homeowners banks went on the attack against it silently and secretly. They needed it declared as "Google Attorney At Law" the insider name given to self help websites that prepared homeowners with knowledge resources to challenge mortgage securitization in foreclosure matters. Despite the fact the Go Fight Foreclosure System 2.0 worked for many homeowners to challenge foreclosure enforceable security interest. Still there was a strong demand to say it was all nonsense and anyone who followed any of the information was a fool. The homeowner who challenged foreclosure by researching online was indeed practicing in Why? Well, the one thing I did was to cover myself thanks to the assistance of some of the most powerful brilliant legal minds in the world who helped me and focused me on how to protect myself to provide this powerful knowledge to homeowners. See I made powerful friends all over the world and I never ever provided anyone legal advice. That would be the one way they could get me and believe me they tried hard to trap me on that one. However, no information product did I ever produce upheld or asserted to provide legal advice or even foreclosure consulting. That's how they got many companies offering foreclosure rescue help and I never even had to advertise.

How strong were their "Google Attorney At Law" efforts? There was even a detail report uploaded to the "American Bar" website about Go Fight Foreclosure System 2.0 being "erudite sounding" which also implicated that it created a false sense of empowerment to a "beleaguered" homeowner. Wow, I thought really? However, their report revealed one groundbreaking piece of the missing puzzle for me and why I am writing this new material that can help anyone struggling with an upside down mortgage today or trying to fight foreclosure. Their report revealed that the Go Fight Foreclosure System 2.0 cannot prepare the self-represented consumer for the intricacies procedure of litigation. That's the word the report used, intricacies...high power attorneys understand this, I am talking about the ones who make millions.

I felt like that was so very true and was the missing link as I did not provide legal advice only the securitization piece of the puzzle. Worst the foreclosure defense attorneys were even more clueless, the homeowner was in trouble. I took the Go Fight Foreclosure System 2.0 off the market and it will remain off the market forever...after I discovered this and I didn't care about the profits it was making! The system was also selling at $299 a unit when I pulled it and had no shortage of buyers it was purchased by many foreclosure defense attorneys, consumer law attorneys, forensic auditors, business people, homeowners, etc. People all over the country and world wanted to "talk to me" about my knowledge of mortgage securities concerning foreclosures.

The most intriguing requests were international homebuyers especially from China wanting to talk to me about U.S. foreclosures related to mortgage securities. Giving the fact that so much property in the United States today is purchased by international buyers it all makes perfect sense now. I always say if you buy any property in the United States you better Quiet Title to the property just as a reassurance you really own it...

I am providing the link that covered the report on the American Bar's website (likely it will be removed soon I waited years to mention it publicly). I didn't defend against the report because in part I agreed with the litigation struggles homeowners face when challenging foreclosures. I was fine with what the report said about the Go Fight

Foreclosure System 2.0 as long as they didn't attempt to attack my expertise or character. Anyone who purchased the system very well know "I" was the one who created it! They didn't focus on me individually just the system....

See the link:

https://www.americanbar.org/content/dam/aba/administrative/professional_responsibility/5_upl_and_mort_foreclosure_fraud_bankers_persp.authcheckdam.pdf

Plus they thought enough to identify the Go Fight Foreclosure System 2.0 oppose to the tons of other sites attempting to cover the same kind of self help information. They even expressed that Go Fight Foreclosure System 2.0 was not the most "egregious" again a high power lawyer term.

My purpose is to put understandable knowledge in the hands of consumers about mortgage securities and detail information that will not require them to challenge their lenders "legally" in court but using Uniform Commercial Code powerful knowledge and of course this knowledge is not to be taken as legal advice. Now smile...

The American Dream Scam

To understand what it means to live "The American Dream" is to understand the setup of Wall Street and how mortgage securities really do work. Wall Street wants you to dream bigger, they want you to get married and start a family so one day you can buy a house. Not just any house but one with envy, a place to have a awesome backyard barbecue...what the heck make it a pool party too. Maxing out the American consumer in debt and taking on financial responsibilities that they really can't afford. This is how most consumers live day to day. When they return home from work it's almost time for kids to go to bed ... Kids are shipped from school to after school programs and curricular activities while many parents are still at work trying to afford the mortgage.

What about buying that simple house with no pool or gated community? Of course it's not generally in a good school district for the kids or a top performing school. It's just that simple house and not at all a reflection of living "The American Dream" or even close to the perception. After all everybody should look like they "balling" (look wealthy for those who don't know) out of control. So for the sake of happiness appearances families buy into Wall Street perception of what family life should be or even look like...they dive in with a big plunge taking on a mortgage loan, most times two mortgage loans a first and second too and even credit cards. After all you need the credit cards for fancy family vacations, you know to post pictures on social media so everybody will be green with envy. Nobody and I mean nobody loves social media more than Wall Street and for greedy reasons.

This may sound alarming but most people really don't understand what a mortgage really is or how close Wall Street is to their mortgage loan. I'm not just taking about people who don't have lots of education or training.

The majority of people don't understand at all how a mortgage loan really works no matter what their background and when faced with foreclosure or upside down mortgages they can't defend themselves.

I learned along time ago that knowledge is power and wealth with knowledge is being very smart. Hence my statement "What Smart Rich People Don't Tell and Big Banks Will Steal To Not Let You Know" the real key to decoding upside down mortgages and foreclosure nightmare. No one wants to uproot their family and have to start all over again in a situation not by choice. Now it's time for homeowners to get schooled and take back their freedom to live their "own" version what an American Dream should be. The world is very diverse and American is made up of many cultures no longer should the perception of the American Dream be a one size fits all.

Lesson 1

For many reasons homeowners need to learn more about mortgage securities and most importantly securities fraud. Ask yourself what is a mortgage?

Most people simply understand an mortgage to be a legal agreement to take out a loan for borrowing money to purchase a home. That's it they don't educate themselves much further beyond that reasoning. Sure they understand that the mortgage payments are spread out by years generally over 30 years to pay it back. They even know that they also agree to a "promissory note" along with the mortgage but really don't understand the differences of these two documents. Some people even confuse them to be one and the same but they are not the same.

At a real estate closing a borrower actually signs a promissory note and mortgage. They are two different documents and have two different purposes. Along with a promissory note the borrower will also sign a third document called a deed of trust in most states. However, in Georgia (always got to be different) the deed of trust is referred to as security deed but same as a deed of trust. The deed of trust (security deed) is not the mortgage and often commonly confused but they are not the same and this is a very important factor when it comes to mortgage securities.

See every Promissory Note contains all the terms of the loan and this document creates personal liability for the borrower to pay the loan back. The purpose of the Deed of Trust (Security Deed) serves as the stronghold to put the house up as collateral for the loan.

When it comes to foreclosure most lenders don't like to foreclose on the Mortgage because there are challenges impacted by flaws in mortgage securities. Mortgages require judicial foreclosure process needing court approval. Whereas, foreclosing on the Deed of Trust (Security Deed) general does not require any judicial procedures or unless the lender seeks a "deficiency judgment" after the foreclosure. So the majority of foreclosures are non judicial and are granted without any court approval to review. How a property is foreclosed on varies by the foreclosure laws of the state, foreclosure will be non judicial or judicial process.

Before You Steal My House

Now that you feel a lot more knowledgeable about the differences between a mortgage, promissory and deed of trust (security deed). You need to understand how fraud can happen with mortgage securities. You should get it now that the mortgage and promissory note are two entirely different document instruments. You understand that the deed of trust (security deed) is the collateral that puts the house up for grabs should the agreement to pay is not honored.

Lesson 2

What you may not know is that the mortgage and promissory with the deed of trust (security deed) can't be separated ever! When theses documents are separated this makes the mortgage (unsecured) but worst it makes the mortgage fraudulently because there was information not disclosed at closing. First off, under 15 U.S.C. §78c Section 10 the promissory is not a security so that means it's not truly a promissory note. Which when dealing with mortgage securities a promissory note can't exceed the life span of nine months and with generally a 30 year mortgage or any note expansion beyond nine months that makes it a security and not a actual note as you were lead to believe which is not disclosed.

So the fraud begins when a borrower signs the mortgage note. Why? Because there is not truly a promissory note document instrument. Plus all these document instruments must be held together and must always accompany each other at all times.

If this is the case, where is the homeowner's cut when the mortgage securities are sold? The homeowner receives no financial benefits, dividends or interest on the mortgage securities profits.

Under Regulation Z a homeowner can option to cancel the security agreement for failure to disclose these terms for violations. Which specifically Code of Federal regulations 12 CFR §226.23 grants a right of rescission. In U.S.C. §226.23 Appendix H identifies what must be contained in the right of rescission letter.

Now U.S.C. §226.23 Appendix H also says it is not applicable for mortgages. However, involving fraud is the exception to the rule and when fraud is involved this vitiates all contracts.

Fraud occurred in violation of Uniform Commercial Code (UCC) because while it was never disclosed to the borrower at the closing on the mortgage loan, the funding source actually belongs to the signer but this is not disclosed. Without the borrower's signature the promissory note holds no validity to be enforceable.

Before a homeowner allows the bank to steal their house, canceling the security agreement for failure to disclose violations this information would be a smart move.

Steps To Rescind And Cancel A Mortgage

People are shocked to learn that they can actually rescind and cancel their mortgage loan if fraud is involved. That's why Session 3 is relevant for understanding what causes fraud in mortgage securities. After being a former mortgage broker with over 16 years of industry experience I learned a lot about the dirty little secrets of Wall Street and the greed that engines the mortgage industry.

Now, if you only want to learn how to rescind and cancel a mortgage without following the knowledge in the previous sessions I strongly suggest you stop and start from the very beginning. It took me many years of training and working directly with mortgage securities sold on Wall Street to gain my knowledge and expertise. I had relationships with the largest mortgage lenders and understood their underwriting guidelines to sell mortgage securities working directly to Wall Street. I trained extensively in mortgage securitization and created many top selling information products in this area of expertise. This is not something that you skip to complete, you need to educate yourself with powerful knowledge.

Lesson 3

When a borrower signs at closing the funding source is also initiated with the signature of the borrower. Under UCC §8-102 this establishes the entitlement right to the funding source.

The borrower is the only one who signs and initials even with witnesses and notaries it's the borrower's signature that establishes the entitlement. This is what allows the borrower a given right to rescind where fraud is involved.

The most common mistake that many borrowers make when attempting to rescind and cancel their mortgage loan is that they confuse the promissory note and mortgage....which is why session 2 is so relevant.

Often a borrower will focus on a produce the note strategy and mistakenly rescind the promissory note. Oppose to properly rescinding the mortgage agreement which is the security agreement the borrower targets the promissory note in efforts of ending the promissory note. However as learned in session 3 the promissory note was not truly a promissory note which was not disclosed. For instance the borrower rescinds the mortgage agreement and cancels the mortgage to take away any standing against the borrower's property. Please don't confuse this with an deadbeat strategy attempt for the borrower to get a free clear title to the house. The purpose of TILA Rescission is much deeper, it attempts to restore the parties to the position they were in before the mortgage was established.

Review the landmark case Jesinoski v. Countrywide, TILA Rescission was upheld in this Supreme Court case because when the borrower rescinds and cancels their mortgage their is NO default on the mortgage!!!!! I repeat there is now no default on the mortgage.

Not intended to be legal advice or acceptance of legal consulting.

Rescind Cancel Mortgage Sample Forms

A borrower can elect to challenge a lender in court for mortgage fraud and deal with the challenges of defending a long court battle. Which could go on for many years or opt to rescind their signature on the mortgage contract for fraud. By canceling and rescinding the mortgage the borrower goes after getting title to the house and payments made on the mortgage loan back with interest including down payments over a lengthy court battle.

Sample

Upside Down Mortgage, Still Making Payments

****

Borrower Homeowner
Any Street
Any Town USA

<u>Sent Certificated and Registered Mail</u>

Date   /   /

To: Lender Name From:

 Borrower Homeowner Name

Re: Loan Number :

Property Address :

Dear (Lender Name Inserted):

I am contacting you regarding the above mentioned mortgage loan concerning the loan transactions which was entered into with (Original Mortgage Lender Inserted). I hereby inform you that I rescind and cancel the mortgage loan for fraudulent disclosure on this transaction and hereby exercise the right under and pursuant to the Federal Truth in Lending Act, 15 U.S.C. § 1635, Regulation Z § 226.23.

This rescission is hereby based on provisions of Federal Truth in Lending Act, 15 U.S.C. § 1635, Regulation Z § 226.23 but not limited to.

I shall continue to make all payments until this issue is resolved.

Pursuant to the Regulation shall provide twenty days after receipt of this notice of rescission to return to all money paid and to take any action necessary or appropriate to reflect termination of the security interest.

Pursuant to 15 U.S.C. § 1640(a) if you do not cancel the security interest and return all money paid with interest within 20 days of receipt of this letter, you will be responsible for actual and statutory damage.

Pending the expiry of twenty days, I am still open to hear any proposals of loan modification including a reduction in principal balance consistent with the current appraised value of today.

Please be governed accordingly,

_____
Borrower Homeowner Name

Sample

Home About To Be Foreclosed On Dispute
Foreclosure

****

Borrower Homeowner
Any Street
Any Town USA

<u>Sent Certificated and Registered Mail</u>

Date   /   /

To: Lender Name From:

 Borrower Homeowner Name

Re: Loan Number :

Property Address :

Dear (Lender Name Inserted):

I am contacting you regarding the above mentioned mortgage loan concerning the loan transactions which was entered into with (Original Mortgage Lender Inserted). I hereby inform you that I rescind and cancel the mortgage loan for fraudulent disclosure on this transaction and hereby exercise the right under and pursuant to the Federal Truth in Lending Act, 15 U.S.C. § 1635, Regulation Z § 226.23.

This rescission is hereby based on provisions of Federal Truth in Lending Act, 15 U.S.C. § 1635, Regulation Z § 226.23 but not limited to.

The security interest held is invalid to foreclose on my property and the tender requested by (list creditor foreclosing)is not entitled to enforce the instrument. Pursuant to the Regulation shall provide twenty days after receipt of this notice of rescission to return to me all money paid and to take any action necessary or appropriate to reflect termination of the security interest.

Pursuant to 15 U.S.C. § 1640(a) if you do not cancel the security interest and return all money paid with interest within 20 days of receipt of this letter, you will be responsible for actual and statutory damage.

Pending the expiry of twenty days, I am still open to hear any proposals of loan modification including a reduction in principal balance consistent with the current appraised value of today.

Please be governed accordingly,

_____

Borrower Homeowner Name

When challenging foreclosure it is always a good idea to send notice to the foreclosure attorney by fax and certified mail.

Borrower Homeowner
Any Street
Any Town USA

<u>*Sent Fax, Certificated and Registered Mail*</u>

Date   /   /

To: Foreclosure Attorney

From: Borrower Homeowner Name

Re: Loan Number :

Property Address :

Dear (Foreclosure Attorney):

I am contacting you regarding the above mentioned mortgage loan concerning the loan transactions which was entered into with (Original Mortgage Lender Inserted). I contacted (list creditor foreclosing) and informed that that I rescind and cancel the mortgage loan for fraudulent disclosure on this transaction and hereby exercise the right under and pursuant to the Federal Truth in Lending Act, 15 U.S.C. § 1635, Regulation Z § 226.23.

This rescission is hereby based on provisions of Federal Truth in Lending Act, 15 U.S.C. § 1635, Regulation Z § 226.23 but not limited to. The security interest held is invalid to foreclose on my property and the tender requested by(list creditor foreclosing)is not entitled to enforce the instrument. Pursuant to the Regulation (list creditor foreclosing) shall have twenty days after receipt of my notice of rescission to return to me all money paid and to take any action necessary or appropriate to reflect termination of the security interest.

Pursuant to 15 U.S.C. § 1640(a) if (list creditor foreclosing) does not cancel the security interest and return all money paid with interest within 20 days of receipt of my letter, they will be responsible for actual and statutory damages.

Please be governed accordingly,

_____

Borrower Homeowner Name

Generally, it is a good idea to call the foreclosure attorney and find out if the creditor claiming a right to foreclose is going to continue with the foreclosure after receiving notice to rescind and cancel the mortgage loan.

While sometimes the creditor will request that the foreclosure attorney still go through with the foreclosure. Many times the creditor will request that the foreclosure attorney cancel the foreclosure after receiving notice to rescind and cancel the mortgage loan.

The effort is to force a loan modification that is affordable or settlement agreement. Even after foreclosing when a notice to rescind and cancel the mortgage loan is received a creditor will often not validate the foreclosure sale which is done sometime after the foreclosure occurred.

Special Training Offer

Continue On.....

If you are struggling to get a loan modification approved, owe more than your house is currently worth, or facing a foreclosure situation....Mortgage Cancellation Secrets could be the solution to resolve all your problems.

Knowledge is power, take control and demand that your mortgage lender works with you.

Quiet Title Fixer

FREE AND CLEAR TITLE

Complete DIY Easy Fill-In-Blank Forms For Quiet Title Action.

STATE STATUTES EXAMINED

Are you tired of struggling with Mortgage Foreclosure Issues that seem to never go away? Do you dream of owning your home Free and Clear? Look no further than our Quiet Title Fixer!

Step-by-step guide provides easy-to-follow instructions that walk you through the entire process of canceling your mortgage using self-help forms.

Buy Now!

https://mortgagecancellationsecrets.com/quiet-title-fixer/

Are you facing a foreclosure sale date? Do you have a Covid pandemic forbearance ending? Do you have a loan modification ending or been denied a loan modification?

Get Tools right now for BEST FORECLOSURE DEFENSES! Get Instant Access!

Forms Expose Mortgage Securities Faults!

Powerful strategies to raise forceful foreclosure defenses and challenge enforceable security interest to foreclose on a property.... Methods to obtain a complete mortgage loan history.....Gain knowledge of foreclosure laws by state, procedures, and more.

Buy Now!

https://mortgagecancellationsecrets.com/foreclosure-survival-swipe-forms

Receive Mortgage Cancellation Secrets Forms and Bonus (Mortgage Tender Negotiation Forms) bundle!

DIY Rescind and Cancel Mortgage Forms with easy instructional preparation. There is no fluff. This is so simple to use and understand.

Buy Now!

https://mortgagecancellationsecrets.com/mortgage-cancellation-and-bonus-tender-forms-bundle

www.ingramcontent.com/pod-product-compliance
Lightning Source LLC
Chambersburg PA
CBHW070229210526
45169CB00023B/1529